BECAUSE YOU PREVIOUSLY
LIKED OR PLAYED

BECAUSE YOU PREVIOUSLY LIKED OR PLAYED

POEMS BY

JIM REDMOND

DEEP VELLUM

DALLAS, TX

DEEP VELLUM PUBLISHING
3000 COMMERCE ST. DALLAS,TEXAS 75226
DEEPVELLUM.ORG · @DEEPVELLUM

DEEP VELLUM IS A 50IC3 NONPROFIT LITERARY ARTS ORGANIZATION
FOUNDED IN 2013 WITH THE MISSION TO BRING
THE WORLD INTO CONVERSATION THROUGH LITERATURE.

COPYRIGHT © 2023 JIM REDMOND

FIRST EDITION, 2023
ALL RIGHTS RESERVED.

SUPPORT FOR THIS PUBLICATION HAS BEEN PROVIDED IN PART BY THE NATIONAL ENDOWMENT FOR
THE ARTS, THE TEXAS COMMISSION ON THE ARTS, THE CITY OF DALLAS OFFICE OF ARTS AND CULTURE,
AND THE GEORGE AND FAY YOUNG FOUNDATION.

PAPERBACK ISBN: 9781646052776

LIBRARY OF CONGRESS CATALOGING-IN-PUBLICATION DATA:

NAMES: REDMOND, JIM, AUTHOR.
TITLE: BECAUSE YOU PREVIOUSLY LIKED OR PLAYED : POEMS / JIM REDMOND.
DESCRIPTION: FIRST EDITION. | DALLAS, TX : DEEP VELLUM, 2023.
IDENTIFIERS: LCCN 2023020568 | ISBN 9781646052776 (TRADE PAPERBACK) | ISBN
  9781646052981 (EBOOK)
SUBJECTS: LCGFT: POETRY.
CLASSIFICATION: LCC PS3618.E435 B43 2023 | DDC 811/.6--DC23/ENG/20230501
LC RECORD AVAILABLE AT HTTPS://LCCN.LOC.GOV/2023020568

COVER ART BY JULIANA TANCHAK
COVER DESIGN AND TYPESETTING BY
DAVID WOJCIECHOWSKI | WWW.DAVIDWOJO.COM

PRINTED IN THE UNITED STATES OF AMERICA

CONTENTS

CONTENTS

CONTENTS

ACKNOWLEDGMENTS

GOD SPEED, MR. PRESIDENT. GOD SPEED.

Goodbyes are always awkward. The president isn't too touchy-feely, neither is the vice president. They don't touch. They don't feel. They just kind of stand there and acknowledge the moment. Mnuchin is a bit of a crier, but otherwise, it's like everyone is already looking back at this special time in their lives. All the great memoires. All the good times. Remember when? Remember when? Well, what an honor it was. I guess this is it then. The president waves to his faithful staff and supporters. He waves to the empty parking lot from the top of the portable staircase. He waves to his wife and son as he boards the airplane. Goodbye. Goodbye. He waves to some clouds. Goodbye. His little face in the little airplane window as the airplane ascends higher into the airspace holding just long enough to see him gently waving goodbye to his own simpered reflection.

THE DARK PHRASE

A woman from a faraway land
throws a shoe at the president
and the shoe turns into a bird
and the bird flies out the window
and it keeps flying over the mountains
until it falls into the hands of a poor boy
who whispers many sad and lonely things
into his hands every night
until the bird turns into a stone
that the boy drops in the river like a wish
and the stone keeps dropping down into the river
into the water into the darkness
all the way into the past it keeps dropping
into the bad dreams of a shopkeeper
where it turns into a dark phrase
they have to write down in their ledger
all of these ghostly transactions
to finally get rid of the phrase
until many years later
when a cleric transcribing the old mysteries
finds the dark phrase in a book
and touching their cold heart
it turns into a blessing
which they give to the downtrodden
which they give to the poor
and the blessing turns into a cry of freedom
which the people beat into swords
to bring down the ruling officials
who had tried to turn the dark phrase
into a cruel edict and the people turn into citizens
and the freedom turns into commerce

and the commerce turns into the shoe
that the first woman threw at the president
which this time turns into nothing at all
as it falls to the floor behind the podium
because there are no longer mysteries
which can touch such a man of this world

THE WAY

There was a wisdom in all things.
A purpose spelled out
in the creep feed of fractals.
The fingerprints of the potter.
The fire in the equations.
Millions of krill riding
the current of *because*.
A way to read your way back to god:
Downwind of the reactor's busted gullet,
the oak leaves still stretched upward
toward some chance of rain.
Some perfect design stitched
into the supervirus, its sepulcher
suspended a thumb's width
away from the permafrost's
melting point.

THE HOUSE OF THE FATHER

She runs her hands through my hair
until it all falls out.

We find a narrow heart line at the base of my skull
which breaks all the way up into the girdle of Venus.

We build a small house along this broken river.

It shakes in the summer breeze.
It buckles beneath the dwindling station of sparrows.

It always appears under our eyelids when we're away
like the press of an empty cupboard.

It points out our flaws.

Sometimes I shirk the law of the father,
but somehow I always find my way home

on these feet that have fallen asleep.
I keep walking backward into her hands

which hold up a Christ child.

I want to teach him to whistle.
I want to tell him the truth:

Someday son, it will be the last days,
and when they ask you what time it is,

they ask for your blood.

But do not forget how your father held you here
for a little while in this house of tiny expectations.

TERMS AND CONDITIONS

Dear Moms
Office Type
Presence of Elderly Parent
Low Educational Attainment and Net Worth
Recently Purchased Civil War Memorabilia
Multiple Credit Cards
Smoker in Household
Multicultural Youth

We build technologies and services
that enable people like you

to connect with each other,
build communities, and grow businesses.

Our mission is to give people
the power
to bring the world closer together.

To help advance this mission,
we may use the information
we receive about you to serve
you content that you may find interesting.

Your privacy is important to us, but

Dear Spousal Benefits, Serving Overseas ...
Marked Yourself Safe at the Jason Aldean Concert ...
Dear David Lancaster, 13-Year-Old Daughter Jessica
Killed in Car Crash ...

did you know that 73 percent of users self-censor
at least once over a 17-day span,

that the mouse hover rate
for the unread messages icon

ranges anywhere from 0.3 seconds
to 12 years,

that we're always devising new ways
to promote shares.

Let baby Jessica,
born March 17, 1999, at 3:24 AM,
know that you're thinking of her on her birthday.

WHAT IT WAS LIKE

We sat in cars mostly
It was like we were children again
We spoke to each other
like we were learning to speak

Nobody loved you
Nobody loved me

You said your own name
in the mouth of this country
never came out right

that you were afraid you were already forgetting
what it sounds like, how to hold the simplest of shapes
For some reason I kept thinking of milkweed
when summer finally hits

My hands passing through whole fields
of its slow sticky bleed all the way back home

When we looked into each other's eyes
it seemed like there was something so certain about me
you couldn't bear to see

For me it was like when I fell in the pond
before I could swim
that feeling you first feel when you know you can't touch bottom

or the one time we walked all the way to the park to watch the sun rise

and when I looked down at my body
I was still there
Only I wasn't
And I never will be again

Our shadows stretched thin as a door closing over those days

INDOOR PLUMBING

When we finally got indoor plumbing, my grandmother was bedridden and would ask for water, glass after glass of it, there was no filling her and no one understood where it could possibly be going. Everyone was waiting, for what, exactly, it's hard to say. To be honest, nobody knew what to make of any of it, but the waiting became important to them, and it filled their lives slowly with a promise until there wasn't such a thing as a life any longer, so much as the waiting and the promise. The slow wet whisper of "more please," that was less and less a voice and more and more what we were realizing for the first time is only the world, and wonderfully so, the waiting to see if after one more glass, all ninety pounds of our grandmother would finally say "enough," or "thank you," "goodnight." And if during a full moon, the children coming in, somehow called by the gentle crashing of the tide, could discern their own trajectory across whatever history trembled beneath grandmother's blouse. And me with my younger brother watching the gentle rise and fall of that blotted entirely, the dark shift of her dropsical thighs, the sleepy children crawling up around her, into the bed, children buoyant with love, and loved back in a way that only water loves the buoyant. Can I cry then and breathe a small prayer across the slow wash of her coming in and out around us all, hoping for the prayer to find its way back to me someday in a bottle or a dream? And a strange gravity pulling the whole house toward her then, pulling the whole town toward her, until everyone had quit their jobs, until all anyone ever heard was the sound of feet running to and from the water faucet, from everywhere and every world, all to one point, all to two words—"more please," "more please." And soon all speech was forgotten or abandoned in the place of those two words. When she finally did die, everyone was still waiting, and the promise, whatever such a promise could possibly be, had become so big and everything else emptied out by it, and we were waiting for her to burst open with it for so long. And when one of the children dropped a penny down her throat, there was no splash, and maybe after the point of departure, no penny either. And once in a while, someone will still carelessly go to the sink with an empty glass.

TODAY IS THE PERFECT DAY

Your mother back home, she says she is beautiful
for the first time in her life;

she has sold the house of her ruin and gone shopping.

Your father has finally forgiven his father,
he shares this with you.

A party: all the pretty girls and all the pretty boys
from your past have gathered,

have pretty things to say

and all the ugly ones too, saying if they only would
have known how beautiful

you really were, how suddenly brave and true.

OZYMANDIAS 2020

I activate a poorly rendered NPC
from gens gone by, who mouths no more
than "America the beautiful!" "America
the beautiful!" "America the beautiful!"
when I select "who are you?" "what year is it?"
"items for sale/trade?" "America," his face's
jerky motion capture locks into place.
"America," when clicked again. "America,"
he proudly gestures to a discard pile
of jumbled graphics. A story mode I've
long forgotten. A great and mighty man,
reduced to a text box's character limit: "I never
said that" half sunk like a cat turd
in the open sandbox's smoldering obsolescence.

WHAT TO WEAR TO THE END OF THE WORLD

Normal was in again.
Or fun, simple colors.

One of the pastimes
was recreational maths.
Abercrombie coitus.

Cutting the cucumber
sandwiches into tinier
and tidier approximations

until they turn into mush.

ARE YOU STILL WATCHING "OLD MAN, EPIC FAIL"?

The office temps huddled round a bright screen.
Their faces held together in the low glow.

They are watching an old man in a field
who keeps pressing send.

They are waiting for something to happen.

And the man in the field is waiting for word
from his son overseas

for over 3 months now
and no answer.

And the word is waiting somewhere between
the bend in the circuit and the break of light

all the way back to his mother's sickbed,
who has been waiting for years.

For what, who can say?

Who can even remember?

How many farm hands pointing home?

How many wan cabbies, the maps in their minds
slowly cannibalized toward some final destination?

How many phones, the phantom suck of a smooth stone?

And the boys in the office maybe wait 2 minutes,
3 minutes before clicking next.

And the old man in the field,

there are hundreds of hours of him,
thousands of hours, buried forever,

0 views deep, on a server somewhere
thousands of miles away from the son's notification.

PRIMATE PROBLEMS

In this game, the Princes is
        supposed
        to save
        Mario.
In this one, the Gorilla has a thing for guys with mustaches.
                Nobody's
                happy.
    How it works is things don't work out, but the game keeps on going.
    A sequence
    of binary code
sputters in the back of each skull like the rusty four-stroke of a lawn mower engine.
                  The
                  pixels
                  01, 01
                  one
                  another, but they never get the one thing
                              they're
                              configured
                              to want.
Mario wants to be a big man, but he's a man in a cage with a woman with the key.
Donkey
Kong
wants
a Mario that wants him for more than his simple tools—the burn of unrequited
                              monkey
                              love
      enough to chuck keg after keg of displacement. Princess wants a Mario that loves
      her
      for her—
the way she can hold a huge hammer high above her head and feel
                      her
                      whole
                      body

ache for the sake of her man. But you can never move them closer
to what
 their coding
  gives fire.
The game does not allow for this. There is no correct key sequence.
       Up
       Up
       Down
       Down
 leaves the player dead or simply unsatisfied.
 Joystick,
  joystuck
on the heart's quick starter. The player is supposed to police
         flesh
         by
         way of
 navigating a few central commands. The player is supposed to favor
 a series
 of slight
 hops
over emotional investment. Even if the player beats this level, there is another,
           and
           another
    another with the same ladders, the same
    gradual
    inclines,
    same
basic controls, but only more intricately laid out—as if the programmers had meant
 for
 this
 infinite
 cruelty to gain gravitas under the system's relentlessly singular assault.
        Always
        a kill
        screen
    instead of the kiss. Instead of backstory,
    an
    ambiguous

platform
with the structural integrity of a soft egg. This is called playing the game.
                                        No matter
                                        how
                                        many
spare quarters, how many new lives ... Even if they all got where
they
wanted
to go,
then what? A castle, a solid 9 to 5 plumbing gig, Sundays at Bowser's, a compromise
                    instead of
                    the high
                    score.

OBJECTS IN MIRROR ARE CLOSER THAN THEY APPEAR

I pay a man five dollars to clean my car with his spit.

He keeps calling me boss.
I keep calling him boss.

We've agreed on distrust as the best option.

We watch each other work over our shoulders:
He is the crankshaft of a cotton gin; I'm a sucking sound
like a drowned vacuum.

His body is an arrow he shot through the world and back
into his bended knee;

mine is the trapdoor of memory:
the trapdoor spider
too fat to fit out.

The legitimate danger in this scenario has
something to do with deciphering the difference
in the other's God-shaped hole;

almost fitting that space before self-awareness,
the regularly scheduled program, interrupts us again.

The commercial says: I'm not a human doing,
I'm not a human thinking, I'm a human being.

In the commercial the man is washing my car too,

but there's a disclaimer:

You missed a spot he says, handing me his face.

CLOUD GATE, CHICAGO

Whatever is given here
is only, instantaneously
a giving back—

a sort of lapsed mitosis
which bends the city
in the easy hammock
of its untiring appraisal.

Or a thing divorced,
polished clean of ideas—
to sit unthinking and alone
in the flat well of its
refracting

or to belatedly recall
quicksilver as a child's
plaything

within its perfect balance,
above suspicion
above intention.

Giant bean,
fat parabola,
the belly of some future
Buddha,

and underneath this all,
a navel,
as if such things could be born
beyond suffering.

NEW SINCERITY

The poem I wrote for you, I don't think it's the right poem.
Or it wasn't really how I felt, was it? It was how I had been feeling

from before, and for a long time, but maybe not now.
It was the poem that kept keeping me there, making me feel

these same things. And it's sad really. Like I could never quite move on
from that one spring when everyone was writing nocturnes.

All my professors leaning in like they had a hot tip
on the commodities index, saying, have you read this or that nocturne,

or have you written your nocturne yet. And I was like, no,
I'm writing my poem, and it doesn't want to be bothered.

And I'm still writing that same poem that goes your hair so long
and let down into the well of some village's drinking water.

Or your glance so dark and impossible like a secret left
open to everyone. And what does that even mean? Wasn't I failing

even now to know what that really might mean? And you, whoever
you were then, all the while, tapping your tongue against your teeth

in some chair in some waiting room somewhere, humming the tune
to *Sanford and Son*, impervious to such things.

It was the only poem I knew how to write I guess.
Or the poem where I was still like 19 or whatever,

smoking a cigarette in front of the Chem building, waiting
for your Intro to Philosophy class to let out, wondering if I looked cool

enough or not. And then there you suddenly were. And I don't think
I know how to write poems anymore. Or I don't think I can ever unlearn

how the poem already was. Or I'm over thirty now,
my greatest cultural insight having something to do with how it's ok

to say no I have never heard of Nolan Potter's Nightmare Band, and I don't
even know where you live, who you are, or where to put this silly

little poem. I just don't think there is much more left to say about any of it.
It's already too late to change any of my lines about changing my life.

MADAM PRESIDENT: AN AMAZON ORIGINAL

The episode opens with Hillary Clinton in the Oval Office. It's one of those alternate reality ideas that writers kick around when a series is starting to go stale or they're too lazy to come up with a coherent storyline. It's mostly just Hillary sitting in a blue pantsuit behind the big desk looking poised. Ready for whatever. Maybe a few flies scroll over her forehead, but that's about it. It was the most salient image ever, one of the data analysts remarked, eliciting some of the strongest numbers we've seen on both ends of the favorability index. A sort of polarized fill in the blank, how easy it lent itself to all kinds of wish fulfillment to just have her stand there like a cardboard cutout. The only real problem is that the actual Hillary might still actually be in there somewhere, spelunking about the detritus of possible Hillarys or simply biding her time by clearing the desktop, filling the birdfeeder, thumbing through a bestseller. Making do with oneself daily. Just like the rest of us. And nobody wants to see something like that. So, we have to stick to the political angle, to keep making the threat of it real, but to give it mass appeal. We'd have to find a way to somehow make her look confident, but also like she's going to fail every time. She'd have to seem sharp, persistent, but somehow powerless. The suffering, I think, if done right, is something both sides will embrace. If we keep hitting on that, then we've got a show.

PLACE POEM

I am told my great-grandfather used to hunt his own land for birds.

The sound of footfall on snow, yes, is a good, old-timey sound
because in it is a crispness the same crispness as the color of clean

decision, an unspoken resourcefulness accountable only to its hard

scrabbled lonesome. Imagine, the huge silence I knew to be that man
making himself smaller in the silence of the world's soft unseens

in order to line up a rifle sight with the fluttered *I want to live, I want to live*.

How close you have to come in on this image to see
him as him, outside the shot, away from the dapple of grouse,

away from the still life with skull, cluster of grapes, Nintendo 64

controller, a man as a man cut free from his known business.
But I am always interrupted by this or that pop song of my own devising.

I am told a vast field of white as far out as our history

will take us. I am told my hands are the hands of family
past, I have never known their faces, measuring the plow horse

all the way up to its eyes, but I am also shown the No Private Dumping

signs gelding the backwoods like this is something that matters,
something I must take with me. I reached my hand into farming

maybe once or twice and what I pulled out was a nonstory.

I looked at it like I might look at the small blank screen
of a flip phone that's been stripped of a SIM card now for years.

QUEER FOLK

this was a one-quarry town   God made it that way

hovers over the face of the deep like a twinkled foreclosure

sometimes I swim there   sometimes I get high and see my face in the water

it doesn't mean much

that was the year we were supposed to get a Walmart
some people say it still might happen

one time I did mushrooms with Jimmy   I saw some regular-sized cows

I was more sick than anything

in the parking lot whose frightened child is this
is a typical kind of question   one keeps to themselves

I think my favorite summer was when Mickey Mantle hit 54 homeruns

that was when I was supposed to sign up for the army
but even that fell through

I think how I see things now

is maybe how my daddy used to say his unenjoyment check just came in

when I go down to the water

where the fathers and their fathers used to work stone

the size of a mammoth's skull   the dumb magic of a Cyclops

I feel the diving lesson that won't take inside me

spitting the drowned Phoenician back up   even what's left

of the shallows refusing   I want to say something

like I am my own ossuary

DOWN BY THE WATER

Two deer come to drink down at the water's edge. The pond is unreal how it won't reflect light. How it holds it all into itself. But the moon is just some kind of typical moon you might find in this kind of dream. Because even in dreams there are purposes, minor points of no interest that hold them together. The floodlight through the trees spilling off from the car dealership. The way that the crickets weave a low canopy, a soft boomerang settled over the heat map. The way that water takes you in whole like this was meant to be is mere physics. And the two deer are actually two dreamers that during the daily routine of cut off your own hands never know that each night they together will drink from the same digital representation of water. That somewhere their double is taking their lunch break alone among the city's blurred passengers. The thing about deer is that they are so present, but passive. This is why dreams keep inviting them in. Because the thing about dreams is that they keep going back over the same things. It's all the same deer down by the water's edge. The two dreamers falling through the same dream like another flesh suit. And the deer do not dream in the dream, because they are real deer and this is as far as things go. And so they are trapped there in something like love, without ever knowing it, which the waters can't help but abandon in this moon's certain angle of studio light.

HOME REMEDY

The president enters my dream life.

His head is a large human head attached to a crab's endocrine system
and carbuncular body.

It's an image I've seen on the internet
after googling the Medieval Clown Tradition too many times.

It's from a hack-and-slash video game version of *Dante's Inferno*
from the early 2000s

where the severed head keeps mouthing *I Don't Know, I Don't Know*
as it skitters choppily toward your imagination.

There are many slippery nodes,
many slunk openings through which a receptive body can pass,

but the president doesn't like germs.

How The Glands of the Human Body — WebMD
begins with *What is a gland?*

Society was so clean.
Most of the undesirable bodies were excised or rerouted,

their bodily fluids extracted from the GDP,
their enzymes blowtorched

out of the Declaration of Independence's saline solution,
blood quantums alchemized into border-crossing statistics.

That's the kind of convenience the president goes for,
the sort of dead entry point he's hoping to stretch over

the yawn of your inner life.

And I don't think he liked his crab body very much,
how it felt, and fit the sphincter of his soul.

How he doesn't like an unwieldy context, the sticky residue
that human contact portends.

The pee tape for instance. The thought of it sliding
into the cassette player's garbled mouth parts.

But this was my dream. The trickle of new life forms
down a long dark leg.

At the bottom, Trump begging for more.

AT THE LEARNING ANNEX

I drop out of night school.
I go to the chop shop instead.

I have things
that need cutting:

a new fang, a sore hoof
for the rasp.

I watch a man in a mask
with one huge eye
wield a small flame.

He calls it the burn
victim mask.

He makes an incision.
All day he does this.

He stands and sweats over
many raw metals.

He strokes a silver tongue
against anything
that will give up the solid.

The eye is so big and black
and fills his whole face
with its unblinking appraisal.

I go back to school.
I have trouble with math

and simple word problems
and the part about which side

declared war
on the other and why;

the part about putting things back
together after

you've broken them down.

SLEEPING JESUS

I was trapped in the other tomb. The one where Jesus forgot to wake up. Slept in so late with a new body too bright to open. Slept inside the soft fruit of Himself with the rock still stuck there like a ball gag, where after four days the disciples stopped waiting and went back to dental school or took up the study of magic, dialectical materialism, the sleep cycles of locusts. Some simply consulted the tides; considered their nets a newborn silence dipped into the old silence of water. They were wet with cold fishy silence, they were dry with the hard silence of wives, they were left to the slow wean of sons. Each night they considered their own sleep and the sleep of others as a transport into His. Here, they started the short-lived Church of the Sleeping Congregation, where each Sunday, tucked close to these truths, they got to sleep in. Some grew tired of this and some stayed at it. Some had strange dreams of a sleeping Messiah: an immaculate bed lifted high up over Israel, from which the Day of Rest would finally be proclaimed. Some couldn't sleep anymore and were considered cut off. Some began to speak abstractly of a total REM state: wherein, a whole waking life could be replaced with the disco light of hallelujahs, the heart burst open with Apache missiles, psychosexual ablution. Each year, thousands began to gather around Golgotha, hoping to sleepwalk their way back to the sealed tomb and awake in unison with Jesus upon their arrival. But none of this worked. He never woke up and we never slept easier.

MINUS 14

All the TVs were stolen out of our house; the void of 14 channels.
At night I can hear my mother's spoon scrape the bottom of a bowl.

The world is that empty.

2

SPECIAL FEATURES

The season opens with the president staring directly at the solar eclipse, pointing, pointing significantly, as if to say look all the way into it.

ONE BIG ONE

I was paired with another boy from the internet.
Our bodies as flat as a Ouija board.

We were supposed to say certain things like globalists

instead of the Jewish problem. We were told
to be here and build togetherness

like it was a game of red rover for keeps.

We were told to Siamese Jesus.
We were each given the same wounds

and conjoined accordingly:

It was called the death of the straight, white man.
We healed into each other.

I was taught how to message board, how to work

an incendiary phrase into the soft targets,
hit post, and reply, and keep hitting again.

At first it felt like gooseflesh

stretched too far over a seesaw, or sharing
an aboveground pool for a personality,

but then the brain's nautilus lost its flotation devices.

My body didn't make sense after a while.
They kept adding more people. I wasn't sure

which one was me, which means it was working;

the collective unconscious
converted into a glitch mob.

Somebody would come and do the same

head count, take a few measurements,
feed us the talking points. Everything moved

by the slow rotisserie of a utility meter

BURDENS OF PROOF

Here is a list of people claiming to be Jesus in some radicalized form or another (these are the Jesuses we really need to worry about).

These are all the police reports involving methamphetamines and the theft of home insulation from the last 15 years.

This is a cross section of malevolent data flow suggesting IP address 96.170.4.8 and source port UDP 19 as a possible spoof point for Guccifer 2.0. It belongs to a Starbucks in Minsk.

This is a receipt from Enterprise for a Honda Odyssey signed for by one of the face cards just outside of Reno. The plan was to just keep driving.

These are the known unknowns. We know them best.

First: Construct concept of identity. Construct concept of them for purposes of constructing concept of us. Construct concept of threat.

Second: Develop method of identification and framework for guilt.

Third: Identify criteria for culpability / threat. Identify individual. Identify individual within context of culpability / threat.

Fourth: Eliminate individual. Never under any circumstances are you to eliminate the concept / presence / possibility of threat …

This is (inaudible). You find him and (again, inaudible, light clicking sound, a sort of sterilization that leaks into the mind's low and fluorescent lighting).

This is what an act of terrorism looks like and this is what it doesn't.

This is threat level alpha. This is threat level omega. It comes in red, orange, and occasionally code midnight.

Know that when no water is readily available, they are permitted to perform ablution by sand. Know that all things are permissible to you in pursuit of them.

In Mali, the average cost to maintain 100 child soldiers is roughly 12 US dollars per month.

In Turkmenistan, a man leans against a wall next to some goats, he turns, he coughs into his hand, he turns and adjusts his waistband.

ONLY I CAN FIX IT

The president can't do anything right, or is it dear leader can do no wrong? He launches too many missiles, not enough missiles, or just the right amount of missiles into the Ayatollah's proportionate reply. He's one of the worst presidents to win so much and keep winning ever. He rails against any number of forgettable names and events, but it's ok because they get back together or become someone new, even bester. It was all part of the show. He told the leaker to leak those things when he was telling him not to do it. Even if he did keep them in cages, wrap them in foil, it was Obama who did that and everyone loved it. He's a master of four-dimensional chess who can barely play checkers. He gave us the how to lurch briskly ahead of the queen, behind your opponent, how to exit any number of international accords, while contracting the camera's pink eye. He told the Chinese to stop fake newsing about climate change. To give us our jobs back. And they do it, because they never did it in the first place, like you wouldn't believe. He chips a bad typo into the weeds of one of his tweets. Poor dotard. But he coins a new phrase. It's called America first. Hundreds of new steel mills. The DOW over 25,000. 256,000 deportations. 217 ethics violations. 27 indictments and counting. It was only Rosie O'Donnell. No, it was not. But what does it matter? Or how to keep track of what the big deal was? Who is Flynn on the phone exchanging sweet nothings with Kislyak for $1,000? Or it was Clinton in the basement of Comet Ping Pong Pizza with the acid-washed emails at the behest of James Comey. The North Koreans dipping a big toe into the DMZ just before the commercial break. The face of George Soros on a food stamp the size of the Empire State Building pointed right at your pineal gland. The whole world watching as the whole world burns before it's on to the next fire. The Finns off in the thick of their forests somewhere calmly raking away.

DARK WEB PASTORAL

I wile about in your wayback's persistence.
I suck all the stimuli out of the skinner box.
I was a son of a son of some horse traders

from when the death of beauty was still a frontier
untouched by the data science.

Now I'm just another dumb kid dicking around
on the dark web, my synapses all sickly
with anarchist cookbook and pokemon card stats.

Now I'm writing a key sequence to set up a botnet.

Now I'm watching some torture porn.

Now I'm on your computer.

I'm sending some malware, sifting
through pin numbers. I'm watching you watch

some virtual yoga vids through your camera.

Your face is so boring.

Your body not good and filled up with fail pixels.
I'm already bored with it
before it even begins.

Watching your daughter sleep unencrypted
via nanny

cam was much better.

The soft mouths of babes.

Impenetrable plaintext.

Using the voice function
to provide reassurance:

hush little angel, don't say a word.

SOMETIMES, A CLOSENESS

Check the front door, the inbox.
Check under the car.

Check the news clips
for missing persons,

irregularities
in eye contact, references

to God's coming judgment.

Check the oven timer,
the baby's breathing.

Consider the tap water's
translucence.

The desktop's low hum.

Know he can find you,

even here.
Sometimes, you can smell the milk turn

sour before it does.

Somewhere, the sound of children laughing.

Try to remember:
I live next to a school.

Look, but all of those swings
are empty.

It seems like a long time ago—
his hands in your hair

like a lot of loose serpents,
he used to

say, like speaking
in tongues

you can never take back,

almost ten years ago
—but, maybe, it's closer than that.

Remember: wet grass
and rug burns,

down on your knees.

A police baton
to the back of the head,

that fuzzy kind of hurt
like the name

of your boy
not even old enough

for you to name.
Already, unspeakable.

It's less a remember now
than a tiny alarm

that you take like a sacrament.

Try to swallow.

Think: *it's not
a very close kind of sound*.

You can't even
check it.

SOMEONE IS ALWAYS ON THEIR WAY

The swivel chair is squeaky in the Oval Office. The carpet has been steam-cleaned until it is a slightly lighter beige. Washington continues to cross the Delaware in the oil on canvas, 1851. Tonight, the kitchen will go with honey baked ham, single serving of mashed potatoes, half serving of vegetable medley. On the back of every one-dollar bill certified by the US Federal Reserve, it still says "In God We Trust." Somewhere in Kandahar, a camel spider has been working the sweat out of a soldier's empty boot for months. In Queens, a child counts the same 11 roaches before falling asleep. Out on the South Lawn, the sun hangs glibly in the threadleaf. Someone is on their way shortly with a cold can of coke.

FALSE FLAG

A crisis actor walks into a school
and starts firing off blanks

fake children falling everywhere
fake blood bleeding out of pile of realistic injuries

flank of cameras
feeling around in the fill light
for manufactured fear

various stunt doubles piling out of police van
to set up perimeter to secure scene

prop bodies positioned next to news truck
poly foam poured into shape of small child piled next to family car

falsified death certificates with various timestamps
floating around on the internet

falsified mother makes MSNBC appearance
falsified information spilling out of her talking points
falsified tears running down second face

facebook fundraiser page set up before incident

same girl in photo is same girl
next to Obama at press conference next day

saying same thing

a body full of bullets is a body
full of bullets is a body full of bullets

WHY DO WE REQUIRE FLESH, BLOOD, AND DISMEMBERMENT TO MAKE REALITY TRUE AGAIN?

The call was to call off the air strike that he called

and it was a very good call

because the numbers were not good

and when the jumble of numbers goes in

and starts making this slurping sound

somewhere at the center of Q4 on the spreadsheet

and the organ machine plugged into the energy machine

starts to retch up or out or back in

that's when he knows he didn't like it, he didn't think it was right

because what was the actual exchange value of the drone again?

That was the important, but tricky, part.

If the drone was identified as 150 million monies,

then how many Iranians was that?

THE CASE OF THE MISSING MOON ROCKS

I cannot conclude beyond a reasonable doubt.
Weather balloons rarely register this part of town.

The waitstaff unable to seat parties of that size, shape,
or "disposition." What does the shooter cop say?

#Pot2Blame tonight at 7. Tomorrow, already another
#TotMom. Who isn't is without question, without question.

What is is anecdotally admissible, but too often
a leaky interior with all the lights left on, in too dark

a manner and skin tone to unsee. Whether it was
argumentum ad lapidem or moving the goalposts;

the fungibility of a 2 Chainz chorus or the glint of misgiving
the width of a welfare check; Col. Mustard's latest imperial

home improvement project or supply-side Jesus
in the FEMA Humvee turning floodwater

into TV ratings … will determine the reader's
affections for the rest of *The Mystery of the Stop*

and Frisk Soda Dispenser and on into I cannot recall how
many times I cannot recall I have placed the placemat

above suspicion, the velvet Elvis beneath the bed.
When required to give a more accurate description,

I usually go with 50/50, ask the audience, or please
consider the wildflowers, how they grow in the wild.

Please select which option best illustrates an argument
for or against intelligent design: A banana

fits the hand perfectly, so does a Glock 17.

DIRECTOR'S COMMENTARY

To see beyond the Terminator (his singularity conceived in hyperalloy, his slow lurch as someone off-screen sweats out a few bars of "you've got me burning," which slips back into a sort of mechanized thump and grind as he nears the camera). To see beyond the point of his trigger finger. To see beyond the bright aurora clouding your exit. To see beyond an end. Is there a point on the strobed horizon or is the gaze beyond gazed into … And I don't want to talk about the Kathryn Bigelow Oscar, what I want to talk about is art, is beauty held up under extreme scrutiny. For instance, what is that look on Sarah Connor's face and is she even the right Sarah? I still can't pin it down. But I keep coming back to it: the knowledge to end all knowledge, a loneliness here (to be the last Sarah Connor and not even sure), a staring into the abyss, which coddles the stillborn reflection of self. Everything slowed down even more so is what I was going for, stretched out through the fish-eye lens; the dilation of that pause with the gun just barely pulled back. I ease into her face here, and I've done a lot for women, a lot of strong roles, and her eyes (deep with knowing, but also shallow with death, a give in the eyes here, not a take) and even her lips, half-pursed, half-opened; a stoic indecision, whetting that horizon. There is a hum; there is a frequency in this closeness I think, a beauty to the beginnings of violence (what the laser connects and what it hints toward): the bright point of death that shines her forehead into recognition. Here, unlike in the other scenes, the shot is never fired.

AT THE DRIVE-IN THEATER (*BLUE VELVET*)

First you get the hunger,
then you get the fear. Frank pulling the car over,
Daddy again:

You want a love letter from me,
do you know what a love letter is fuck,
straight from my heart,
a love letter is a bullet from a gun fuck,
you get a love letter from me and you're fucked forever.

Applying the makeup is a pleasure all its own,
and then to kiss the boy forcefully leaving your mark.

SQUARE ONE

In the parking lot,
under the buzz
of Beer, Wine, Lotto,
I am lighting the cigarette
of another beat man.

The half-drunk Marine,
his sober appraisal
of my shattered handshake.

His *my wife left me again.*
His guttural *damn this*, and *damn that*
as if the work of some broken god

had dragged his voice back
from the desert's big empty,
had tempted a stone into bread
only to harden again,

as he pours some Jim Beam
into his Slurpee. All it takes
is for him to hand me
a swig, straight from the bottle,
straight to the brain, the whole spun
world I have punched into
every night shift, every blue hour

where I am only consolatory,
where I am only a cashier
with a name tag to prove it.
My *hello, how may I help you?*
I can only make change,
and am only sometimes
clever enough to remember
that two sums of money
are distinguishable
only by their amount;

that each man, finds out his own
separate damning, in due time,
the remainder of which we spend
seeking it out in each other's.

THE CONSPIRACY OF ART

Even the local public access channel has been commandeered by the government. George W. Bush is on the 2 AM time slot leading a class on art therapy called American Exceptionalism: 1945-2004. There's a few muffled coughs, a soft, wobbly shot of him smiling, legs crossed on a stool next to a canvas in front of his students. "Let's start with watercolors," he says, "something domestic, think of a peacetime scenario, it's the simple observations, some little strategery of birds or something, that I like to start with. Don't overdo it, and don't try to force it. But don't misunderestimate your own talent either. Just think of those little birds and then you just let your feelings guide your brushstroke on the follow-through." He shows the studio audience some of his work. A man's soft body in a bathtub. A man's soft body in the shower. A man's soft body being barked at by a police dog. A cup of coffee on a kitchen table.

"And you know," Bush continues, "a man, when he's president, he has to carry a lot, there are things that he can say and things that he can't say about the things that he knows, that he's done, the things that he thinks, and they weigh on him hard—like after he's done with the job. I think war is a dangerous place, for instance. That air pollution is polluting the air. That it's a time of sorrow and sadness when we lose a loss of life. That what's wrong with the French is that they don't have a word for entrepreneur. And so, when I'm painting my little birds or something like that, that's what I'm trying to say and not say. That paintings is where wings can take dream."

Now it's time for the students to give it a try. Obama is thinking of that dress Michelle wore to the inaugural ball, but he gets lost somewhere along the way trying too hard to get her arms right. Nixon is stuck sweating over a seemingly infinite sequence of lopsided filing cabinets. Reagan has an idea for an experimental piece called "1,000 Points of Light," but can't seem to configure the right ratio of rugged individualism to corporate welfare. W. looks slightly befuddled as he walks by each student, but maintains an encouraging tone. He makes his way over to Trump, who is still sizing up the blank canvas like it's some kind of threat, a betrayal or catastrophe waiting to happen. He remembers some of the stuff Bush said about the freedom of expression, American exceptionalism, all the beautiful things. He leans in a little as if on the verge of a breakthrough, hesitates, then takes out a gold Sharpie and signs his own name.

NEOLIBERAL INDIFFERENCE

I'd been reading Immanuel Kant again, mostly for style.

And I liked how he looked almost kindercore on the front cover

as I held *The Critique of Pure Reason*

over the soft toss of my face

on the University park bench.

Like I was a student.

Like he was thinking all these svelte thoughts in a rigorous way.

And I liked where my mind goes when I see the big words

like a posteriori and ontological imperative.

How the ducks were in the duck pond,

kerplunking about.

And the clock tower saying the time is the right time.

And the sun trundled down on the south quad,

shinning over the good and the evil alike.

And the thing-in-itself already gone off

after all the little things that need thinging.

And I feel that enlightenment feeling once more.

LOOKING INTO ARISTOTLE'S TOMB

Material conditions trickled between history and myth:
skull fragments, marble beneath thousands of years of accretion,

50 coins forged to the likeness of Alexander the Great, once meant for wishing.

What still remains ... Now absence of altar is presence of what?
If all men are mortal, and Aristotle is more than mere flesh,

then ... back into the brindled deluge of raw data

to again wash the bald head of knowing with doubt.
To touch each worn particular in which the universal still blinks ...

To point to a place on the body and say soul ...

To point to the dirt and say everything that is earthly. To point
to a place on the map and say we have found the remainder

is to know your own way of knowing is best.

Empires expand and stretch themselves cool along the lines of their own
unanswered questions. What still remains is written over. A palimpsest:

some desperate mix of learning and animal need; a treatise on rhetoric

is erased with a patrician's plea for more money, more time.
From the first hardened shibboleth of western civ

to the IMF's humdrum assessment of Greece's forever financial crisis,

there is much ephemera that is now of little value.
Empirically speaking, history provides no bailouts.

That there is evidence that this is the actual tomb of the great philosopher,

over 2,000 years forgotten, is not enough.
And what is not enough only keeps going in all these derelict directions.

One implication might be an uptick in national pride.

Another the vague renewal of interest in metaphysics. Someone suggests
an increase in tourism revenue. Someone sees the skull fragments

and considers the cost of production for 50,000 bobbleheads.

IT CAME TO PASS

It's a made-for-TV movie that starts with *The LORD was displeased*. There's a lot of foreboding. A darkness like the darkness not seen since the time of Barack descending over the heartland. And through this God saying to Trump, take now thy son, Don Jr., thine only beloved son, and make haste to the house of corruption, the house of Pelosi, and build there an altar and make ye a burnt offering unto the Lord. For the Lord, your God, is a vengeful god, demanding blood for blood, but your God is also a god of forgiveness. At first, Trump's leaning toward let's cut a deal, but all of this business about sacrifice and walk ye in all the ways of the Lord god who made you makes him uneasy. He gets Giuliani on the phone instead, who sends Lev and the gang to Jerusalem to dig up some dirt on this God guy. Turns out his son was a real loser, some sort of communist flunkie, palling around with prostitutes, money collectors, various scumbags. Trump decides to take things up a notch. He has Rudy make the rounds on the Fox News circuit. He fires off a few tweets: I like the messiahs who weren't captured and crucified and #Where's Jesus? along with an image of a dark, empty tomb. He keeps bringing it up at his rallies and press briefings like "look, this is a guy, he's a very bad guy, acts of sedition, practicing medicine without a license, assault of a public employee in a place of worship. This is serious stuff. A very unstable guy. I mean weeping in the Garden of Gethsemane? Weeping? In the Garden? And this is supposed to be God's only begotten son? I don't think so." And it seems like it's working. Sure, the sun is swallowed up by the moon. And the shadow of death digs deeper down into the grain. And the poor and the hungry cry out. But they've fired Mel Gibson, and brought in some guys from Cambridge Analytica to do a few rewrites, and from here on out Tim Allen will be playing God.

TELL ME THE STORY ABOUT MONEY AGAIN

I think it's a poem

every time the eco feminist
stabs the venture capitalist in the neck
with a letter opener

and all of this money comes pouring out

and the norm core capitalist turns into the gore capitalist

because money is fungible like that
it makes many things happen

because money moved at the speed of information or
money was the new information

and you couldn't remember what happens next

because all of the money filling
up the whole screen

but in a fun, flouncy, full of life kind of way,
this flotilla of dollar signs,

and you tried to cover the money hole
with your hands covered in money

and the children, there were always more children

and they were the future

gurgling up from the internet's jittery scree,
so smooth, without countenance and incontrovertible,

saying please tell us the story about money again

and I was wrong about it being a poem
and you were wrong for what you've done
and the children were always right

because all they were asking for
in their innocence
was only the kingdom of heaven

POEM LIFTED ALMOST ENTIRELY FROM THE BILLIE EILISH EPISODE OF *HOT ONES*

On the screen was like an anime, it was just walking over or whatever
I lifted my arm up and she lifted her arm up
and it was like automatically copying the thing
The idea is you get to each other and you get to each other
like really little like
squeezed into a cute little there's nothing left over
and then you hug and that's the whole game
What it's called is what would a Billie Eilish horror movie look like
or I used to be like huh, I love hate but now it's more like
did you guys talk about anime and sneakers without me again
That's the thing they're doing right now and
we try to say stuff that doesn't have to
be that deep; it could be something random like I feel sad and
I don't really speak Japanese and he doesn't speak English
but that's ok
because I think we're finally getting somewhere because this was when,
remember, we were trying to say stuff that doesn't have to
be that deep; it could be something random like I feel sad and
suddenly I'm alone in my room
and jaden smith comes down with a big ass Cuban link
and he starts touching my foot and he says I'm healing you

FINAL FANTASY 45

Pale sorcerer appears.

Attack with purifying strike, heavy mallet, arrow of light: 0 damage.
CNN: attack with news coverage: 0 damage.
SJW: attach with justice, truth: no effect.

Pale sorcerer casts tweet, retweet: 200 damage.

Average voter: attack with apathy, confusion: -150 life.
Party official: select regroup, select new messaging.

Pale sorcerer counters with wall, wall, petrify.
Pale sorcerer casts drain the swamp: manna is drained 50 points.
Casts plausible deniability, gaslight: poison effect activated.

Party official: select potion, potion, switch out player.
Celebrity: cast charm, public outcry, charm: heart increases 5 points.
Intelligence agent: attack with incriminating evidence:
pale sorcerer's agility reduced 25 points.
Court system: select lawsuit, lawsuit, impeachment: no effect.

Pale sorcerer summons shadow troll: troll, expert troll, whataboutism: 100 damage.
Pale sorcerer summons guileful minion.
Guileful minion attacks with disseminate, alternative facts,
disseminate: 250 damage.

Party official: counter with Biden, Buttigieg, Klobuchar, Biden.

Pale sorcerer attacks with KAG hammer: 750 damage points each.

The party is defeated.
Collect 0 EP, collect $0, previous save file corrupted.
Play Mario Party instead.

FINAL PRESENTATION

What was the whistleblower really trying to tell us or what was
the difference between a crime and a crime-like behavior,
quid pro quo and just palling around, or what is the meaning
of life, or death for that matter, while I still have you here,
45 more minutes left of class, and already the silence creeping in?
And I wonder, is it really just one, or are each of your own silences
a unique pinprick, a number on the diabetic test strip,
showing the blood sugar of this great "American" condition?
As Michael Foocoo might say, I've watched *Forest Gump*
three or four times now, but it only makes sense of its own time
if *you* see it on VHS [my emphasis]. I guess I have an old way of seeing,
shot through with Red Bulls and Mario Kart,
that this department continues to deem unsatisfactory,
but when the professor explained the emotional limits
of kitsch, how it created a new kind of silence in art,
and which way could we possibly go from here,
I thought, perhaps the indigenous peoples of Halmahera
(where approximately half of the population is now Muslim
and half Christian) we briefly mentioned three months ago
could teach us something more true about our national impasse.
Perhaps we should be thinking in terms of the Wikipedia page
for *Being and Nothingness*. Perhaps the difference
between ritual and politics at these or any other fine Subway locations
will help us refine our thesis statement. But before I begin,
I would first like to tell you about my scholarly method,
which I've taken mostly from my third-grade teacher telling us
to free write about corn for hours every day, her eyes all homogenized
like a warm glass of milk, as she led the grand march
across the school year, slowly filling up a large map of Michigan
with the paint of our tiny handprints, where instead of The Pledge
of Allegiance, a moment of silence was to be given each time
we were told to look upon our own works. Should we not first give
that same knowing look here, along with whatever that vaguely

Nazi-sounding guy's name was from somewhere deep in the dregs
of our course pack, knowing too that there is nothing
outside the text? Should we not "dash," as one of the core objectives
on the first page of the syllabus indicates, "a few Lacanian mirrors
against such rocks, braid a Plato's beard or two to Thelonious Monk,
sneak a little Caesar into our word salads," with those same small,
unwashed hands we started out with? Sure, such and such an approach
could be said to lack any real reference to the means of production,
the modus operandi, the meat, the potatoes, but at least I have
some handouts of the first giant panda to give a live captivity birth
in over 20 years that you can look at before I move on to
the second slide of my PowerPoint on this very important topic.

3

DEEP IMAGES

fell asleep again reading *Paradise Lost*
in a field of unmarked police cars

my mother off breaking
a small horse in the distance

she says her name is pulchritude
something about God's solar plexus
clicking away like a Geiger counter

water lilies bled out in the water's slow wizen
and what are you doing way up here
second-guessing all this garbled creation without any gloves on

she bends the pony's head into a bright star
but this isn't the right dream either

I Ctrl+Alt+Del, Ctrl+Alt+Del
all over my own face

swaths of chartreuse, red dye #40
sucked from under my eyelids
spit back into a pool of basic commands

I'm holding some kind of animal's clean spine now
a bag of loose mercury
a bucket of arrowheads

instead of a map on a screen
I say *Lord, what is all this stupid shit*

I try to rebuild
the tree fort from when I was a kid

where there are no longer trees
where a water treatment plant
now spins its dull spell work

I write childhooddog.exe, firstcommunion.exe
sunsetovercastlerockaftercrossingmackinacbridge.exe
nothing happens

I write in the space where it says
do not write in this space

everything I've wanted to say for so long
passing over the hillside's autocorrect

FEED

We looked at the sleepy pile of puppies

We looked into the lizard's long eye

Listened in on the dark sire of crickets

Watched a scorpion balance its cruel rosary
on the flat back of its skull

And the older boy glancing over his shoulder

at us like I told you so

when we got to the tank filled with feeder mice

We all knew what was what

We all maybe wanted it at least just a little

We all always do

how whatever had brought us here brought us anywhere

boredom, bad grammar, the cable TV finally cut off

How a few firecrackers can manifest at any moment

How carefully a boy's hands can work
in the shadow of that circle

How gently they tie the things of this earth down

How it's always the weakest boy that has to go first

Something about suddenly hating in yourself what you see in him then

How the word *pussy* passes from one mouth to the next like a kind of open sesame

How quickly a voice screaming *don't do it*

goes all the way back down and down deeper into storage inside you
and just sits there forever from that point on

And the smallest boy almost crying as he leans over the little stupor of mice

looking back at us all like the jaws of life for maybe a second

and all of the other boys laughing along with the crackle and pop

and I didn't say anything, I did not look away

LESSONS

One of the things that my dad tried to teach me
was about waiting …

like when we were at the good Kmart, and he bought me the new Creed album

but said I had to wait two frickin months for my birthday.

What I learned was that waiting doesn't work nowadays;
that that was a lesson for some long-ago time

because Creed wasn't cool anymore when I finally unwrapped the CD.
Someone found out they were vaguely Christian, from Tallahassee
or something.

And I started to worry
that maybe Creed was never cool to begin with,
and if I couldn't see that back then, then maybe I didn't get it.

It was terrible.

But it was also going to be ok, because I started listening
to Tool just in time.

SHIRTS OR SKINS

This was when I wasn't sure
if I was a boy any longer.

I couldn't wait
any longer. I had to start walking
toward the woods.

I came to a great stone;
big obsidian quiet
by a whole field

of magnetic afflictions
strung out to dry
under a sentinel hum.

Tall trees, I felt them:
toenails curled under
the toe, wet coils of pubis.

I could not make out the image
the stone wished to make for me,
but felt it wanted to make it.

Someone had washed
this certainty away

in a rain over
seamless dead skin;

a dark pit, sweet calloused center;
hard candy stuck in the throat.

The stone could have fit the palm
of a giant perfectly, the stone

could have at least given me
a fingerprint. I tried

to find an opening,
but there was no way into it.

Under the trees,
there were piles of salt.

No. They were people ... once.
Powdered milk poured out

of missing children
—words like the dry
hiss of a gas leak

or a jewelry
box of old coins—

with the faces bald and worn
off the carton
but some of the dates still there,

last seen 1984, 92, 95 ...

LATTER DAYS

After high school there weren't any jobs.
So we took to burning mailboxes, entire newsstands,
an old Buick Skylark
finally lit up like the true American god
it was meant to be.

What had started out as a matchbox
and the collected works of Anne Sexton—
we didn't even know who that was, what it meant,
we will never know how any story goes
even now, because every time we try
to think of anything, we think of fire,
that match, those pages,
the back seat of a school bus
when we were 12 ... Anne Sexton,
her name like a district burned over
in the fat of our minds as the bus driver
pulled off to the side of the road—

And when you're as young and dumb
as we were, everything is a fire waiting
to happen, and your brain
is the malted black of a King Cobra bottle
tucked tight between your thighs
in a brown paper bag
as you pass a patrol car;

drunk on your own bad thinking
and the bad thinking of friends
burning you all the way home
to a family cut down to canned goods
and cigarette butts. The slow hum
of a ceiling fan measures itself
as the day's only wager.
Here, the center of the world
is your father's heavy wrist, without
a single task or blame before it.

HAGS

Sun in the eye
bends the periphery into Schrödinger's cat;

other minor difficulties you can't make out
with.

The insights tent-pegged into the skull

flag-gun like billboard,

suggest

more schizophrenically:

36 oz for $1.99.

You try to interfaith with this,
but it's hard

when all your decisions are poorly
punctuated

freight trains in heat,

summer plus boys,

can't solve for x in the shape of suicide door kits.

Your mood goes right
through you like baby food.

Thought travel like a tan line;

a large-print bible ruined in the wash.

The same

pugilist under Apollo's persistent reach
punching holes in the logic

through which to view the sun more directly;
to see at least and say *oh, it's a dead cat.*

BASIC HTML TAGS FOR 2000S PARENTS

```
<html>
        <head>
                <title>15 Things to Know about Your Teen Being on the Internet</
title>
        </head>
<body>
```

<h1>underage teen even</h1>
<h2>more underage</h2>
<h3>on the social media</h3>
<p>i.e. preservative <br /> chemical compounds <br /> reduce risk

 of microbial spoilage <br /> but how underage <br /> is ok
 fit for the flit of five-second
 Snapchat <br /> or maybe other
sharable Panopticons <br /> for American prosperity are <br /> to be
suggested <br /> screen says <br /> text too much texting <br /> to dear
LISTSERV <br /> for automated yes</p>
<p><audio src= "while Dr. Phil theme song.mp3"/audio>
 does
pastiche of Maury Povich's <br /> mix of hyperreality and hot flashes of
scientific inquiry <br /> with new sincerity <br /> about choking game

 on latest Nielsen <br /> prefab feels <br /> arrive in Q4 asunder

 the corporate monad <br /> into survival mode <br /> care mods

 <img src="derpette.bmp"/>
 because <br /> to invent the
teenager <br /> was not enough <br /> when going to free market
 without proper ad specs <br /> or InDesign proficiency <br /> was
too YouTube bucolic too <br /> now teen comes in <br /> off-white
 <image src="whiteguywithbackwardshatgivingthumbsup.gif" width=1
height=2,000 alt=WhiteGuyWithBackwardsHatGivingThumbsUp"/>

 Dubstazz (which recent Marketing <br /> just quantified
from 5 New Music Genres You Need to Hear in 2015)
 classic
I Can Haz <br /> or SSRI equivalent <br /> but goes into
 Siri
voice <br /> saying *I'm sorry*
 I'm not able to connect right now
so fast <br /> nowadays <br /> your fauxstalgia <br /> can't Shazam
whatever it was</p>

<p>not all plans available <br /> on all devices <br /> but with upgrade <br /> family package <br /> can more <br /> readily track <br /> the remaining balance <br /> between law and desire <br /> which allows
 PornHub <br /> to barely 18 <br /> as most likely <br /> search result <br /> for switching <br /> from baby monitor <br /> to side hug <br /> into Forever
 21
 some breaks are <br /> commercial <br /> mixed use <br /> my residential unit <br /> keeps sublimating <br /> into Candy Crush invite <br /> frequently asked questions <br /> include
 #myteen is a four-and-a-half-star teen
 <image src="amazon.com"/>
 streaming 24/7 <br /> with enough likes to know it</p>
        </body>
</html>

DREAMCAST

Where was I going with any of this? The terra firmer kept ovulating under my feets. I long for those crash bandicoot days when the edge of the map was still a reminder you could wub up against. All of that unincorporated blue slow-dawning itself into distance as a means of a mood or perspective, some kind of soft break between game play and self-actualization.

Nowadays nothing is separated. Nothing is finite. It's all mostly slippage, the gurgle of open-source code eating into the story mode. But it's also overdetermined. That single reticulate surface, on which every possibility had already been rendered. The flit through any infinite number of untenable characters side questing their way for hours into some home equity loan on their longhouse in Windhelm was never unique to your own little player's wants.

Kill shots at least used to be one dependable means of checking one's progress, a reminder of how a single life can be spent, but even then, the body continues to respawn even more elsewhere, away from the through line, with no in-between instead of somewhere near the start of the tutorial.

ALL RULINGS ARE FINAL RULINGS

I was king for a day.

I felt like a glass box
with exactly $3 inside,

like I showed up to the water shortage
with two 10-gallon toilets;

a kind of publicity stunt
that can't be undone:
the latest public housing expo.

I was given a gold chain to wear

I couldn't see past: a flimsy
quintessence; the body of Christ

dangled in front of a motorcade
like a carrot; a self-portrait the size

of a howitzer I was told to preside over,
to garner distrust.

I spit proclamations
like sunflower seeds courtside

at Caesar's Palace; commissioned
an airport terminal from my head

to my heart, a Slip 'N Slide from my ear
to my tongue. All of my thumbs-down

were final, my thumbs-up less certain.

The people said I needed
to conquer something substantial.

I decided to conquer the trends.
Everything I touched

turned to Auto-Tune.

GREETINGS FROM THE WORLD'S LARGEST TIRE

Rubbernecked into the revolving door of itself. Infinity plus one. Material conditions: polyester resin reinforced with glass fiber. Cultural significance: polyester resin reinforced with glass fiber. *Surface against surface producing no fire.* Not even enough recognition to wonder at the means of its enormity, but only to know it again instantly, unavoidable—12 tons of tire—as the unnatural wonder of this world I've returned to. Dear Michigan, your monument does not require an on-ramp, an exit, a national endowment for educational merit. It says, fuck off already, you're home again and that's about it. Fun Facts: This monument prefers to be called the titan's doggy paddle instead of the gatekeeper of Detroit. Serious Facts: This monument is the image of utility too large to be of any use. It makes me feel nostalgia like my stepbrother just sat on my stomach because he was bored and already tyrannical. It makes me feel religion like a millstone sunk back up to the surface. Stuck somewhere in the travel brochure between the state fossil and the state wildflower, *See*: this monument, the immovable state object; the null set that dances against the fist of Joe Lewis. *See also*: Failed fortification of our own failed mythology, we fall under the welcome sign of your grace at 75 mph. Dear failed monument, otherwise known as the Uniroyal Giant Tire, you could have been a thesis statement like 1-800-CALL-SAM, the starship pulled out from Elijah Muhammad's skull cap, an old testament written in the night sweat of teamsters. Instead you daily say you'll be ours like you really mean it: a Ferris wheel filled in with asphalt and storm drain installation.

DISCOUNT TIRE APOCALYPSE

he was on meth when the police caught him
they asked him if these tattoos mean anything
he said warriors tattoo their noses sometimes
they asked why was he breaking into a tire shop
he said that he thought it was almost Christmas
that he needed something good for his little boy
had they seen his little boy how big he had got
when they told him what day it was he laughed
out of kindness like they had told a bad joke
he said the mind is a snake handler groping
for the dead lizard that had swallowed us all
last Tuesday just like some tear of black sugar
and there was no going back how his eyes were
two negatives stuck at the end of a movie reel
burning the ghost of a tired Tom Joad back
into their flashlights back into each brain cell
lit up like a funeral pyre and let go on the water
the ease of the holy spirit slipping the world
back into tongues as they read him his rights

EVERYTHING MUST GO

I found the fire of myself inside of myself.

It was there the whole time;

only, it wasn't a real fire, was it?

It was a stuffed toy at the bottom
of the big claw machine that I'd been avoiding.

100 palely loitering Jesuses mixed in with the fire
like a bad fruit salad
in the time of free beer and motley.

You can't catch a fire with a claw,
but you can catch its fire-retardant representation.

I wanted to win it for me,

but it wasn't that easy, what with the gaunt cotton Jesuses,
the claw, and the clunky controller.

Up close, the fire was even less of a fire.

It had a no-slip grip.

It was machine-wash only.

It came with a list of poorly written instructions.

It had a voice box you had to squeeze a voice out of.

It said I was a bad person.

Why didn't I write my mother more often?

I wasn't a risk-taker, was I?

That I was always wearing that stupid hat.
Why was I always wearing that stupid fucking hat?

That it was a phony fire because I was a phony man
in a world where everything
was either coin-operated or rendered to Caesar.

EXEGESIS OF CROW

The dove goes out and it comes back dutifully. The spirit of God descends like a dove, not like a crow. The crow is a going, not a coming back. The crow does not end in olive branches. The crow is unclean but beautifully and blackly so. The crow seeks out the carrion and stays there because of blind devotion, not because of duty. The crow does not call out after the third denial like the rooster, but hides itself within its own heart grown fat with the solemnity of worms, private worship, many cold stones the color of stillbirth … crow as big as a bread box, packed full of plucked things … crow as big as the hand spread open for Hamsa … wearing the tight hair shirt of itself, crow: a bad little itch inside the larger scratch of a murder. Crow revisiting the biblical marginalia only once to poke out the eye of a thief. The dove—an erasure of light. Crow—because things keep longer in the dark.

E MOTHERFUCKING T

ET keeps phoning home, but nobody answers.

At first you're happy to let him stay,
but then he just doesn't leave.

He picks up the FM on his fat pointer.

He watches the same John Wayne movie
72 hours straight without blinking,

recites entire excerpts from *Baywatch*
and the Reagan inaugural address in his sleep.

He regularly checks in about fluoride levels.

He starts saying things like my bad,
Charlie don't surf, where's the beef,

like do you know who I am, I'm E fucking T,
and we're out of Sunny D again.

Even the guys in the hazmat suits
seem to grow bored with him.

They say he's ruined the alien for everyone.

He gets a gold tooth. He delicately taps
the tip of it with his grouper's tongue

whenever you suggest he maybe look for a job,
consider counseling, even a night class;

it's the only thing left of him with any shine in it.

He says his real work is just starting.
He says he's never felt so human.

NATURAL LAW

Now I'm taking a wrong turn.
Now I'm taking another.
It's too dark to see any of this.

Now I'm in the bad part of town.
I feel like doing bad things.

I don't know what I'm doing
but I'm doing it.
I don't know where I am.

A group of young boys
comes closer. They can't
be older than seven.

They are trying to whistle
but they don't know how yet.

One of them is wearing
a rabbit's foot sucked
clean to the bone.

A long scar like a feather
runs the length of his arm.

Another is tracing his smooth chin
with the tip of a cigarette.

I say, I'm not supposed
to be here. Please tell me
where I'm supposed be.

One of the boys has a face
just like Jim's when he was
younger. How's Jim, I try

to ask him, have you talked
to Jim lately. I need to know.
Please. It's been so long.

The boy looks the other way
and cringes a bit like it pains him.
I can't see his face now.

I can't see anyone's face.
I can only feel the bald
outline of them watching.

I'm still wearing my suit
and my tie. It feels so tight.

Somebody says, let me show you
something. They hold me upright
and they start to show me.

There are many broken
and abandoned things.

It's a strange and terrible place.
No. It's my old neighborhood.

They take me into my old house.
But it's not my house anymore.

Someone has pissed in
all the corners. The smell
is strong and true and sad.

My bed is still there.
I try to lie down but I don't fit.

The boys want a story.
They hold out a book
but all the pages are missing.

HARD WATER

your name was a debt fragment
you had to read right to left

alone to your own

rent-to-own devices;

the tiny foreclosures' addition

right up to the crease of it:

a bloodline like a book
mark settled in the buyer's guide.

*

the republic's last aperture;

linear has lost all residency with you.

the large black sofa sinks into itself.

there is nowhere to sit.

you stand outside
of the one vote allotted to you.

*

some nights you can't sleep

require a more imperial membrane

salt trespass
your say, short of foetal

takes time-released capsule

takes facial indeterminacy

to have gotten this far through the yearbook

to drunk dial all your old dirigibles again

to hang up
without having your say

so big in that sky

*

in this dream a police presence.

you search
every emptied room from your childhood

with a dowsing rod.

you can't even remember

what it was you were looking for.

everything left

the way it wasn't.

the TV starves itself on the same channel.

less itemized now than …

maybe a notebook, a faulty CD,
a few strip plugs;

the slow stave of memory:

the things you forgot to turn off,

a nightlight with nothing
to shadow.

*

instead of the titles and deeds,
tiny claw marks in the impeccable

wood grain.

inside the display case
you don't find the display.

*

as one flashlight tags the insides of another

you have seen your own scrutiny

mechanically separated.

how do the young loves do it
when it's time for goodbye?

two clicks for no and then the total darkness.

+1 269 217 6231 HAS LEFT THE GROUP

At the bottom of the group chat we build a small fire.

We feed it ourselves, our fingers stretched thin

in the shadow of things said. Our bodies

still glinting with data points. We watch a few memes,

a flimsy reply, photos from the trip to Mackinac Island

slowly faltering now

through the spin of their half-life into flame.

The crackle and catch of all this soft architecture

we've called our story lifted over

the edge of the aspect ratio.

And your face through the fire, and the fire

in your eyes looking right through me,

is the last to go free.

ACKNOWLEDGMENTS

For all my friends and family, wherever you found me, however you helped me along the way.

Many thanks to the readers and editors at the following journals, where the following poems first appeared:

Anthropoid: "Primate Problems"
Blackbird: "Hard Water"
The Boiler: "Final Presentation"
Fields: "All Rulings Are Final Rulings"
GASHER: "Deep Images" and "Home Remedy"
Hardly Doughnuts: "Basic HTML Tags for 2000s Parents"
Inter/rupture: "HAGS"
Juked: "Queer Folk"
Leveler: "Discount Tire Apocalypse"
NANO Fiction: "Sleeping Jesus"
PANK: "At the Learning Annex"
Pleiades: "Natural Law"
Raw Paw: "E Motherfucking T"
Reality Beach: "The Case of the Missing Moon Rocks"
Redivider: "One Big One"
RHINO Poetry: "Cloud Gate, Chicago"
Sixth Finch: "Neoliberal Indifference"
SOFTBLOW: "Burdens of Proof"
TYPO: "Shirts or Skins"
Weave: "Sometimes, a Closeness"
Word Riot: "Greetings from the World's Largest Tire"

Photo credit: Iqra Shagufta Cheema.

JIM REDMOND is the author of the full-length poetry collection *Get Back to Work* and the chapbook *Shirts or Skins*. His poems have appeared in *Blackbird*, *Hayden's Ferry Review*, *Pleiades*, *Redivider*, *PANK*, and *Diagram*, among others. Born and raised in Michigan, he received his MFA from the University of Michigan and a PhD in creative writing, poetry, from the University of North Texas. From there he lived and taught in Lahore, Pakistan, before moving back to the US.

Printed in the USA
CPSIA information can be obtained
at www.ICGtesting.com
JSHW050335130923
48423JS00001B/1